LIMEN

Susan Hawthorne

Art by Jeanné Browne

SPINIFEX

Spinifex Press Pty Ltd
504 Queensberry Street
North Melbourne, Vic. 3051
Australia
women@spinifexpress.com.au
http://www.spinifexpress.com.au

Cover design and typeset by Deb Snibson, Modern Art Production Group
Typeset in 12 pt Bembo
Made and printed in Australia by McPherson's Printing Group

National Library of Australia
Cataloguing-in-Publication data:

CIP
Hawthorne, Susan, 1951-, author.
Limen / Susan Hawthorne; Jeanné Browne, artist.
9781742198606 (pbk.)
9781742198552 (ebook: Kindle)
9781742198583 (ebook: epub)
9781742198545 (ebook: PDF)
Browne, Jeanné, illustrator.
A823.3

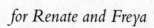

for Renate and Freya

PROLOGUE

a cormorant goes fishing
silver splash
of fish in her beak
the water a still arc

buzz of dragonflies
then
silent as a snake
it's periscope up and
periscope down
traversing
sky air water mud

kookaburras gather
for their daily laugh
on the banks of the Einasleigh

how we bare ourselves
into the sweetness
of sand mud and time
it's birds again and yet again
our ears ringing with
possibilities of laughter
and sorrow

tongues
unforked for renewal
muscles unwound
ready for life's next pounce

3

DAY 1

woman 1:
the river is a necklace of pools
it grapples its way through the land
like a badly executed parting of hair

woman 2:
three years we camp in the same place
the landscape is rearranged
Devonian rocks abrupt against sand

our inner landscapes are changed too
that first year grief-filled for our old dog

on the other side of the river
a black spirit dog arrives
sniffing the Styx
she stands
looks our direction
wades in, drinks and leaves
when my tears—

a bee leaves its sting
in my finger

woman 1:
that first year
we watch the other side of the river
longing for the space to be filled
but spirit dog is gone too

ants devour an old bird carcass
a kite contemplates prey from a leafless branch
the kite swoops the carcass

late in the day a wind drift of butterflies
echolalic laughter of kookaburras
in the melaleuca
its paperbark ruffled
as a frilled ballgown

woman 2:
sorrow lifts in the second year
with you
four-legged friend
dog-paddling across the river
your tail a rudder
your mouth a wide smile

dog:
last year I showed you
my puppy swimming style
you held me in your arms

woman 1:
we raced across the river
me with a head start
you catching up
wriggling slippery as a seal

woman 2:
this year
no water where previously we had swum
in easy nakedness

thunderclouds gather
on the horizon

DAY 2

woman 1:
rain poured all night
by morning the river has risen
six to seven feet

we drive to town
the river is tumultuous
torrenting through the gorge
roaring across the road
bellowing beneath the railway bridge
I walk across
stepping sleeper to sleeper
like a tight-wire walker
my red umbrella above

two men in a car
tell us
you can drive across
the railway bridge

depends on experience
says the big one
eyeing his wiry friend

woman 2:
back at camp
we make lunch
talk in the dampness

remember the wild pigs last year
their grunts and squeals
coming through the dark

woman 1:
I remember the gunshot
shouting our presence
shivering with fear
the pigs' eyes shining
in torchlight

woman 2:
the silence afterwards
the night's tranquillity gone

woman 1:
sunset
a pair of fantails is foraging for nested young
a black-backed ibis mines sand for food
kookaburras echo around and above us
each call passed along the river bed
bounced to a nearby tree
then crackling silence

DAY 3

woman 2:
overnight
the river fills
where yesterday
sand swam in shallows
today is fast flowing

dog:
you throw sticks
I jump into deep water

woman 2:
by the river
her dog eyes follow me

restlessness
sniffing likely eats
swimming again
head underwater
and a flash of fish missed

dark creeps up
the fire whips up in a breeze
then settles
coals build
as we eat camping gourmet
spicy beans tomatoes
topped with yoghurt

the night is easy
softened by fire warmth
and a star-filled sky

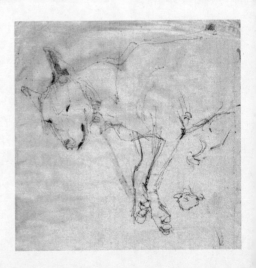

woman 1:
dream
my mother and father
drowning
in ooze of mud
dam building

he driving
she sitting beside him
on the caterpillar
yellow metal
drowning in yellow ochre
bubbles rising
liquid curry
machine and bodies sinking
sinking so slowly
I have time to wake and scream
until the next time
I have this dream

DAY 4

woman 1:
water sodden ground
the river has risen
but below the level of last year
all the same
disquiet bumps at me

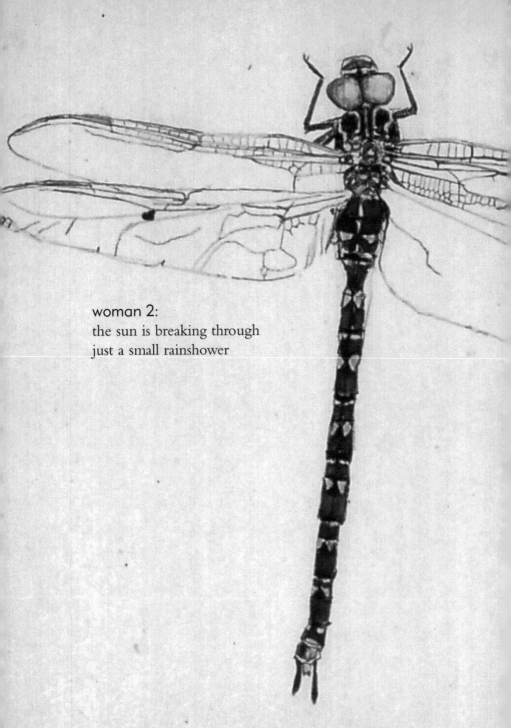

woman 2:
the sun is breaking through
just a small rainshower

woman 1:
how far will the river rise?
when should we leave?

will it be mud-dark?
will the car drive
up the hill?

I'm roadbuilding in the rain
the new long-handled shovel
and wet sand

in the muddy tyre tracks
I make sand heaps
in case of a fast exit

dog:
I prance
into the ochre pool
splash yellow bubbles

woman 2:
dog and woman are soaked through
both of them
rain wet and river wet

woman 1:
from my bed in the car
I watch the water rise
inch by inch
doze
wake
another foot of rising water
a stroll in moonlight
along the sand-strewn track
hope against hope
that the rise slows

dog:
I stretch out
alongside
your nervous body

woman 1:
sleep avoids me
my head pops up
I watch the fireplace stones
my marker of water level

then sleep drops in
takes me
until light
plunges down
the stones visible
sleep again

in my ears
the roar of an old river
this one small
but fear says
small schmall

DAY 5

woman 2:
a figure on a bridge
insect walking
six-limbed
the frame could lift
flutter
fly in circles or zigzags

the railway bridge again
a fuming river
bubbling brown below

the feet of this figure
an umbrella?
a walking stick?

the figure waves
a praying mantis
the world's face in rain

woman 1:
we swim
the dog and I
out into the flow
her large leaf ears
sticking up
I'm racing
she's winning
the fastest dog on the block

woman 2:
we gather sticks
for burning

watch hot coals
spectral colours
quiet conversation
time just to sit
ponder
wonder
what the new year will bring

DAY 6

woman 1:
river water rises by stealth
night terror
wake to no edge
look for the river
it's gone
moved
beneath us
the water's edge
under the tyres

woman 2:
edging out
food boxes are standing in water
it's wet
it's dark
it's past midnight

woman 1:
pack everything
leave everything
stop panicking
pack everything

dog:
you lift me
put me in the front seat
stay

woman 1:
driving into terror
knowing the mud that waits
knowing the sand small-piled
against so much wet

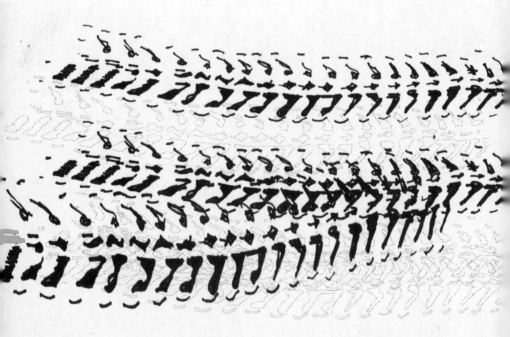

woman 2:
first segment okay
up over sand

second segment okay
onto rocks

third segment okay
more rocks and rising

fourth segment
she's on track
pointing up the slope
and—

woman 1:
keep high on the left
turning up the slope

and then
      the slip
      slip
still turning up the slope
and sliding

no
not there
all sense of direction
gone

woman 2:
the car stops
an awful lean

mud curls around
the stilled wheel

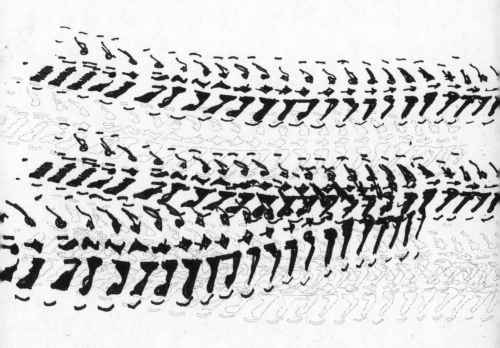

woman 1:
every muscle tight
start
rev
every spring
release
move
still

woman 2:
pile sand behind the tyres
rocks
more sand

reverse

woman 1:
start
rev
release

nothing

woman 2:
reverse

woman 1:
start
rev
release

nothing

woman 2:
her head rests
on the steering wheel

woman 1:
I give up
too much mud
too much angle
too dark
too wet

the river crossing
the railway bridge
the pub
three kilometres

woman 2:
she's walking around the car
her T-shirt rain-spattered
panic in her shoulders

we make camp
just a hundred metres
from where we set out

the car hangs in space

dog:
I wait
in the front seat
of the car

wait
wait

woman 2:
we sling the tarp
over river jetsam
held with vine
and plastic ties

my waterproof
picnic rug on the ground
doonas pillows necessities
the dog settles in the corner

woman 1:
cold swallows us
devouring our bones
night crawls
our bodies press tight
every muscle in tension

dog:
I sleep
curled paws
your body warm next to mine

woman 2:
exhaustion wins
sleep is fitful
I wish for daylight's cadence

when it comes
the rain stops
we sleep in the silence

I wake look around
see the level of the last flood
it could come through
here
        right here
                where we are

now panic surfaces
            gets me up

woman 1:
we eat breakfast
while the rain's in pause
it's only pause

dog:
I have a stick
I run
where is she
this morning
my stick thrower?

woman 2:
we walk to yesterday's camp
look for the red bucket
floated away
in the first quiet surge of water
the dog bowl too

dog:
my ever-filling bowl
gone

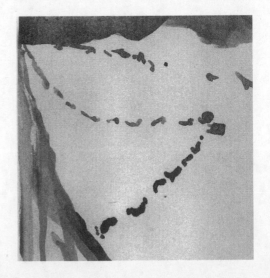

woman 1:
how far will the river rise?
rain pools in the tarp
and drips
another layer of plastic
long sticks like tent poles
holding it all in shape

the doonas are sulking
the pillows squelch
only the dog seems at home

woman 2:
will anyone come this way?
it's holiday time
I worry my own worst scenario
revisit the river litter
holding up the tarp

it really could come this high

woman 1:
I am worrying my own worst scenario
the river rising again
faster
I mull over last night's
exit errors

dog:
I dig a hole in the sand
crouch
ready to play

woman 1:
we sit in silence
watching the drips
listening to rain
wishing for feathers

woman 2:
she undresses to go out
into rain
every dry thing is precious

at 9 am she says
good scenario
it rains until midday
then stops
and the sun comes out

woman 1:
silence again
how many more rain drops
how many days will we sit
in this place
with its dripping sky?

woman 2:
the broken umbrella fixes
the final hole
    for now

the tarp is arched and pegged
tied and plugged

she is sitting with her red pashmina
like a wound around her naked body
even wet it's warm

woman 1:
worse than my last worst scenario
the river rising with a great roar
pouring down the valley too fast for us
we scramble to the hilltop

I'll take my pashmina with me
if we have to leave in a hurry

woman 2:
she tells me her fears
only now do I understand
her wakefulness
her restless checking of the river height

I am counting what counts too
what to take
together our mental disasters
are like an expanding
galaxy of worries

a splinter of sound
I can hear a car

woman 1:
I'm up and running
no T-shirt
no shame

they see me
I go back
pull on a raincoat
walk to the car
the raincoat gaping

dog:
I bark
run at them
the big guy ignores me

woman 1:
he's saying they'll pull us out
scratches his head
we move the camping gear

the wiry one
backs down the slope
attaches the chain

starts
revs
pulls
it moves

reverses
revs
pulls again

he creates tracks in the mud
his tyres scouring a path

revs
pulls
and the car
is moving

he gets out
scratches his head
says *I need a longer rope*
back soon

woman 2:
galaxies of worries
are diminishing

woman 1:
the angle is not much better
still bogged

dog:
you have a stick
throw it
I bounce into action

woman 1:
they return
the wiry one behind the wheel
the big one beside him
this rope should do it

I watch again
his car at the top
ours still down
and then
movement
and the car is pointing
up the slope
it trawls through mud
swallowing air

it sits on the flat
next to the road

they leave to check
their cattle
before the road
becomes impassable

woman 2:
the river is still high
we repack the car
walk to the crossing
feet sink into mud
decide we'll go the other way
dry everything in the sun
have lunch
part leftovers from dinner
we drink coffee
from the damp packet

woman 1:
doonas pillows wet nightwear
cover the rock pile
sizzling in sunlight

a bush laundromat
on ancient rocks

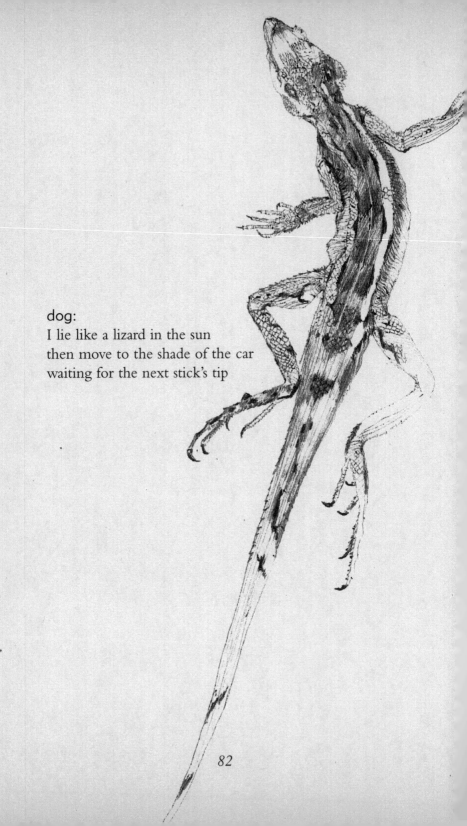

dog:
I lie like a lizard in the sun
then move to the shade of the car
waiting for the next stick's tip

woman 2:
the men return
their cattle all okay
I'm asking about the road
the one to Mt Surprise

just a couple of crossings
you'll be right mate
he says
and they take off
across the floodway
the one we don't want to cross

woman 1:
I'm trying to pull back
my confidence
bundle it tight
after last night's slide

the first twenty-three
kilometres are fine
that's what he said
they've just been there
and back

I'm taking no chances
second gear keeps you safe
keeps you from the slide
into the unknown

I'm thinking about how he slid
into the slide
how he carved an open space
through mud
until he could drive over it

old advice in my mind
keep to the centre of the road
even puddled
it's firmer than the unpuddled sides

dog:
the car jumps
and bumps

no back-seat sleeping for me

woman 2:
water over the road
in dozens of places
muddied centres
potential slides
two creek crossings
deep but narrow

woman 1:
the adrenaline of confidence
is in me
I accelerate in all the right places

a sign ahead
ROUGH SURFACE
that's okay
I can do rough surfaces
it's river crossings that do me in

up the hill
around the corner
and ahead
the widest river crossing yet
I hope for shallow
get out to walk it

woman 2:
I don't think so
it's fast
it's deep
it's wide

dog:
I'm in the river
swimming
water-swift

woman 2:
like fretted strings
we rebound between
two rivers too high
the sun still shining
tympanic clouds are gathering

woman 1:
we're on the flat
high above the river

dog:
sardines for dinner
what next?

woman 2:
dinner cooked just in time
rain pounds down

dog:
there are bones nearby
I can smell them

woman 1:
sleep comes faster
even in the rain
but panic wakes me
three hours later

woman 2:
now what?
how will we get out?
how long?
I keep silent about these new worries

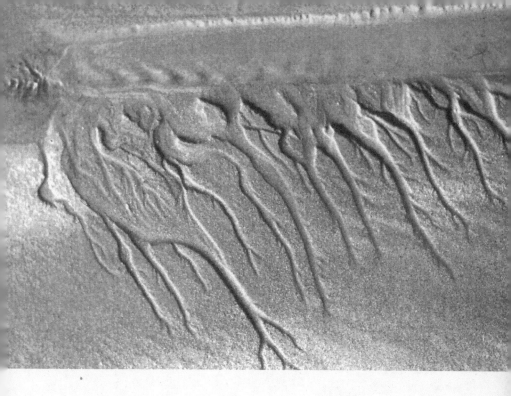

woman 1:
rain keeps falling steadily
rivulets begin at the car's
back tyres
a ribbed knit of earth

DAY 7

woman 1:
the sky is grey
the rain has stopped
breakfast is easy
almost the last fresh fruit
woof and warp of water webbing

washing up
sorting wet from dry
gathering clothes to river wash
dry them while the sun shines
in the never-ending battle
between wet and dry

dog:
they throw sticks
I splash out
swim into the current

woman 1:
a morning dip
sandbanks like oblongate ears
skirt the river
with overhanging eucalypts

return
make the only decision possible
stay with the car
enjoy the silence
the beauty of the bush
mountains
river

woman 2:
I can hear a car
she runs down the slope
with the dog

woman 1:
can't see anyone
I'm halfway across the river
blue ute
one figure
two figures
young tall
they wave
cross the river with the dog beside me

dog:
I'm barking at these two boys

woman 1:
they are brothers
one says
glad we're not the only ones out here
the elder one says they arrived last night
no food

I say
you want some eggs?

woman 2:
they work at the mine
silica
eight of them
it's back along the way we came
yesterday

they crossed three more rivers
the last they needed their winch

we sit in worried silence
none of us has an answer
but four people and two cars
doubles our chances

dog:
I sniff
twenty long toes

woman 2:
so you start work tomorrow?
the older one says yes
and the others
how do they get in?

maybe chopper them in?
I see your face light up
we could leave the car here then?
mebe

108

woman 1:
we could drive you to the mine
and maybe the people with the chopper
could come back and get you across
the two of them nod

they've finished the fried eggs
and silence is like a blanket
if we're all still here tonight
come back for dinner

they leave
walk off like saplings all loose limbed
we sit and read
in the chirruping morning air

woman 2:
the day passes
the sun burning down
I feel inadequate
immobilised

woman 1:
I float feeling the wash of water beneath
arms extended like billabongs
never quite reaching the itchy point
where mosquitoes feed

the river is a psalm
singing like a full-throated choir

could my arms
be jabiru wings
in slow beat
coming in to land?

the dog interrupts
my river poems
kisses me
insists I play
she runs in wild circles
to the water's edge
she is a crazed runner
jumping and turning in the air

dog:
late afternoon
we all go to the river
paddle float sit on the bank

you throw sticks
the big one sinks
you find it
throw it
I run and swim
the stick sinks again
you can't find it either
break me another
throw it

we are sitting on the river bank
I smell the rain
we go back
I shelter
under the car

woman 1:
the rain is falling
in big drops
I am wet through
close all the windows
watch them fog up

time for dinner again
rice and two kinds of beans
for the dog
rice with her tin

woman 2:
she's gone to the river
to tell them to come and eat
she thinks shyness
might keep them away

woman 1:
halfway across the river
I see them again
hard in the twilight edging dark
they say they've found
a winchable crossing place

DAY 8

woman 1:
magpies chortle in the pinking dawn
stretch to light

I'm sitting under a tree
creating the world
as I pick dirt out
from under my fingernails

woman 2:
rain fell all night
the mud looks squishy
building between rills
an entire river system
in aerial view

breakfast is a steamy affair

dog:
this cow carcass smells better
every day
salivating
hungering
chewing
on tendons

woman 1:
back to the river with the dog
it's risen overnight
the two boys are wading through
hip-high water
it would reach my waist
and the current too fast

the older one says
we're going to walk to the mine

you'll need to eat breakfast first
this mothering unnerving
we'll drive you as far as we can go
without getting bogged

woman 2:
you have water?
enough?
sure?
food?
here have these

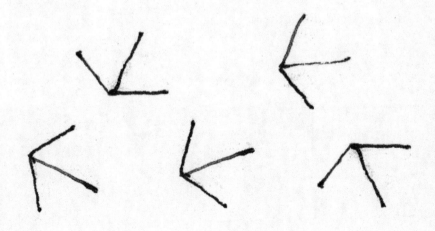

woman 1:
the car is filled with bodies
and paraphernalia
I turn the car and we head back
in the direction we came two days ago

the first water we find is deceptive
it looks flat as paper
but gives the car and all in it
a great jolt
like clear air turbulence

the dog is wedged
between them
on the back seat

the first creek crossing is smooth
the road still puddled
GRID / ONE LANE says the sign
as we turn down the hill

woman 2:
you have to watch this one
says the older brother

woman 1:
I stop the car
and we all pile out
to see if this one's crossable

I remember it
we dropped down into the creek
coming the other way
going back it's a wall

I imagine us sitting
in the middle of the creek
as night falls

too dodgy comes the younger brother's
assessment
he's hardly said a word in two days

we'll walk from here
we can take a short cut past the lagoon
this is my father's country

are you sure you have enough water?

we'll go past the lagoon
I know this country

they are itching to go

woman 2:
worry galaxies return
they are breaking the first rule—
stay with the car

but they are locals
the older brother's lived here eight months
he knows the lie of the land
like the back of his hand
he knows his way
there are two of them
they are young and fit
there's food rest and phone at the other end
they carry with them
their bush knowledge
carried on down the generations

I know this because yesterday
he told her about the birds
the ones that indicate water is nearby

woman 1:
we watch as they disappear
into the trees

we return to the car
and find that things have been flung
out the back
the clothing box
what else?

I hope it's not face down
in that last creek
neither of us speculates
on the other things missing

woman 2:
in an accordion of ever-diminishing
tracks
we drive back the other way

no clothes in the creek
one kilometre a T-shirt
in the middle of the road
another kilometre
there's the box and contents
strewn flotsam on the road

woman 1:
it was that first tiny
water–across–the–road bump
that did it

we gather up the clothes
(a rag bag)
unspoken about spilt medicines
(phew)
the ladder
and the broken dog bowl

in the back
everything is wet
why?

woman 2:
track back
to the uncrossable creek
with its walled exit

another flat spot
to camp
treeless
visible
from the road
and the creek below

together we set up
poles
make shady doona awnings
settle into our camp chairs

woman 1:
the mattress in the back
is covered in water
another box broken
everything out
to dry

nothing has spilled
the water is brown
that second creek crossing
after the jolt
water whirring up from
the back wheels

woman 2:
the sun is hot
worry galaxies nudge her
those boys are walking in the heat
I say to myself
there's plenty of shade
there's water on the way
there's the lagoon
they are carrying water
yesterday they walked
five kilometres upriver
to find a crossing
they walk all the time

another reverie begins
what about us?
do we have enough food
for the dog?
no cans left
what can we ration?
when to start?

woman 1:
staying in the shade
is a battle

from the road
our car looks inviting
with its green
and purple awnings

we survived
the wet and cold
now to get through
sun and heat

woman 2:
we remake the bed
turn the sheet
brush away sand
doonas and pillows dry
looks like new

we read
sleep
wake to needling pain
of prickly heat

woman 1:
we walk to the creek
lie down on gravel
cooling our bodies
outside in

downstream
a white heron
fishing time

135

dog:
I find
a fish to hunt
a stick to chew

woman 2:
water caresses
gurgles at me
we lie here
bathed in uncertainty

uncertainty mars
the magic of the heron
the bubbling stream
the chewing dog
the cooling water

woman 1:
it's a struggle
between the bliss
of this stream
and worry plagues

should we have stopped them
from going?
they'd have gone anyway

woman 2:
the prickly heat
has subsided
washed away

dog:
I sniff dinner
beans and rice again
what about sardines
or that roadside carcass

woman 1:
we bury half the dog's dinner
she's unimpressed
so are we with our meal

have they arrived?
are they eating at the mine?

woman 2:
the wind has changed
warm northerly
brushing our bodies

climb into the back of the car
the dog has finally learnt
the ladder method

we cheer her achievement

woman 1:
look
mud on the roof
that's the creek water

the warm breeze—

DAY 9

woman 2:
during the night
the wind stiffens
cools
more rain
I mull as I back into sleep

woman 1:
at sunrise
clouds are crocheted close
threatening

I walk down to the creek
has it dropped?
a little
the wall of rock
on the far side is visible
safe to cross?
uncertainty edging around me

woman 2:
the heat is rising

woman 1:
cows graze
close to the car
the dog is all
ears nose and eyes
when the cows see us
they stand a moment
meditating
then trot off to join another
who's moved on
they head away
in single file
through the trees
and vanish

like a sign from Chamundi Hill
the red threads
circling our wrists
these cows a sign of luck

148

woman 2:
the heat is rising
and we are back in the creek
it's not yet 10 am
and sweltering

a car
we leap from prone
water-hidden postures

she is running
and the dog with her

standing arms akimbo
in the middle of the road
in the middle of the creek

dust tails appear
then two cars
good news
a woman driving
the front car
and the second too

149

woman 1:
we are meeting and greeting
and I'm telling her
how long we've been here
how the boys walked off yesterday
how we wish we knew when to begin
budgeting the food
and no we hadn't yet

the dog is wagging
her whole body

woman 2:
can we follow you out?
we'll just pack everything up
come with you
it won't take long

woman 1:
she's like royalty this one
with her very own consort
and tough
like my mother
competent
knows the area
says we made the right decision
to come this road
it's impassable the other way
I've got to get to Canberra

car packed and we're off
trailing in the dust of two cars
past the first creek
past the mid-road jolt
back to the hill above the wide creek

woman 2:
out to check its level
it's down since yesterday
perhaps even below
our first encounter

she knows this creek
knows the best way through
leads the way
now stuck but we are pushing

on the other side
she removes her
pale blue crimplene pants
only girls she says
is back to push if needed

next her daughter
in the second car
if she makes it
we're fine

woman 1:
all the adrenaline surging
we're in low low
we're getting there
ourgh
stuck
reverse
foot down
keep it down
revs up
they're pushing
and we're moving
to the other side

would we have made it
without that push?

woman 2:
not the last she says to us
there's one and then another
the second has quicksand
sometimes

I can feel my stomach roll

woman 1:
through the first small creek
it's narrow and shallow
up the rise and past
a picnicking pair
I stop tell them
no point going that way
follow us

woman 2:
at quicksand creek
we scan the water surface
looking for the
lacuna

woman 1:
she says we should go first
why?

because you're most likely to make it
and in that car
you can haul us out

the crimplene pants are off again
she's ready to push
we grind through the water
and through
and through
and we're heading up the slope
and we're across
and I'm lifting from the seat
jubilant

woman 2:
our crimplene friend is driving
she's stuck
but now there are five to push
we're all heaving and pushing
she's across

we repeat it with the daughter's car
and then the two strangers
our crimplene queen
is feigning modesty
but we give her majestic treatment

woman 1:
on our way
no more back and forward
between rising rivers
no more waiting
for sun or rain
or wind to turn

dog:
I have my spot
in the back seat
it's dry

woman 2:
Mt Surprise
one milkshake
two chips
three hamburgers
no onion on one

no police on duty here
we tell the store owner
about the mine
the chopper
she says
yes one was due
this morning

dog:
I smell food
mmmm meat
wolf it down
more—

woman 1:
Mt Garnett
two police on duty
the CLOSED sign
on the door
but I can see them
I knock

I'm explaining about the boys
the officer
the white one
doesn't seem to care
he says *it's their*
problem if they're
out there

the other one is listening
says he knows their parents
says he'll follow it up

I say nothing
our eyes do all the talking

EPILOGUE

this tiny crack
in our lives
wind and rain strewn
stranded on the limen
that space between
water and sky
rain and sun
cold and heat
where we could
be on both sides of time
span beingness
like the unfinished arc
of a bridge
is closing

the birds
the ones that indicate
water is nearby
perch in
the eucalypts

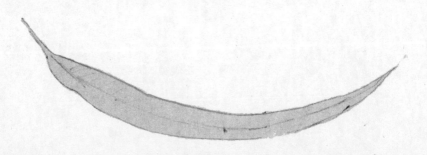

ACKNOWLEDGEMENTS

Several sections of this work have been published previously (in different forms) in *Poetrix* and *Island*.

Nicholas Walton-Healey

Susan Hawthorne grew up in the Riverina region of NSW and writes fiction, poetry and non-fiction. Her poetry collection *Cow* (2011) was shortlisted for the Kenneth Slessor Poetry Prize in the 2012 NSW Premier's Literary Awards and was a finalist in the 2012 Audre Lorde Lesbian Poetry Award (USA). Her work is often concerned with the environment including her novel *The Falling Woman* (1992), her political commentary, *Wild Politics* (2002) and her poetry, *Earth's Breath* (2009). She is a publisher and Adjunct Professor in Writing at James Cook University, Townsville.

Other books by Susan Hawthorne:

FICTION
The Falling Woman (1992)

POETRY
Valence (2011)
Cow (2011)
Earth's Breath (2009)
Unsettling the Land (with Suzanne Bellamy, 2008)
The Butterfly Effect (2005)
Bird (1999)
The Language in My Tongue (1993)

NON-FICTION
Wild Politics (2002)
The Spinifex Quiz Book (1993)